We Dream of a World...

Written and Illustrated by the Gifted and Talented Students
of Pershing Accelerated School in University City, Missouri

ISBN 0-439-36887-1

12 11 10 9 8 7 6 5 4 3 2 1   00 01 02 03 04

Printed in the U.S.A.   08

First Printing, July 2001

Meet the Authors
We Dream of a World ...

Front Row – Left to Right:
Kelvin Carrawell, Ranell Cavitt, Earl Johnson, Kourtney Davis, Jahi Eskridge

Middle Row – Left to Right:
Lakiesha Washington, Timothy Shepard, Marcus Coleman, Rodney Brooks, Jasmine Davis

Back Row – Left to Right:
Astridia Dean, Auja Kelly, Alexis Jamerison, Ms. Hameeda Qadafi

SCHOLASTIC INC.
New York   Toronto   London   Auckland   Sydney
Mexico City   New Delhi   Hong Kong

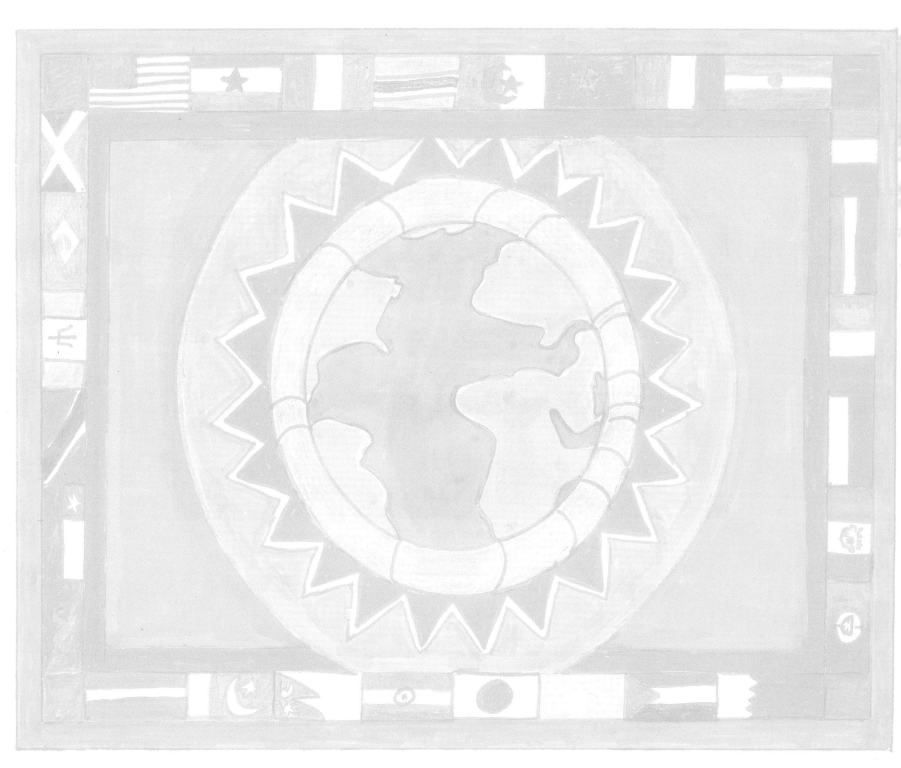

We Dedicate our Book
to the World ...

We Dream of a World ...

Did you know

That there are many, many people suffering from hunger in the world.

When rivers and lakes dry up, farming stops and then people starve.

What Can You Do

With the help of your family or a school organization, donate food to a food shelter or volunteer your time to help at a shelter, preparing and serving food.

Encourage your family and friends to learn more about what they can do to help world hunger.

...Where there is no HUNGER.

We Dream of a World ...

Did you know

There are millions of people in the world who live on less than $1.00 a day.

That's less than $365.00 a year. Can you live off that?

What Can You Do

Donate clothes, blankets, toys and schools supplies to a homeless shelter.

...Where everyone has a HOME.

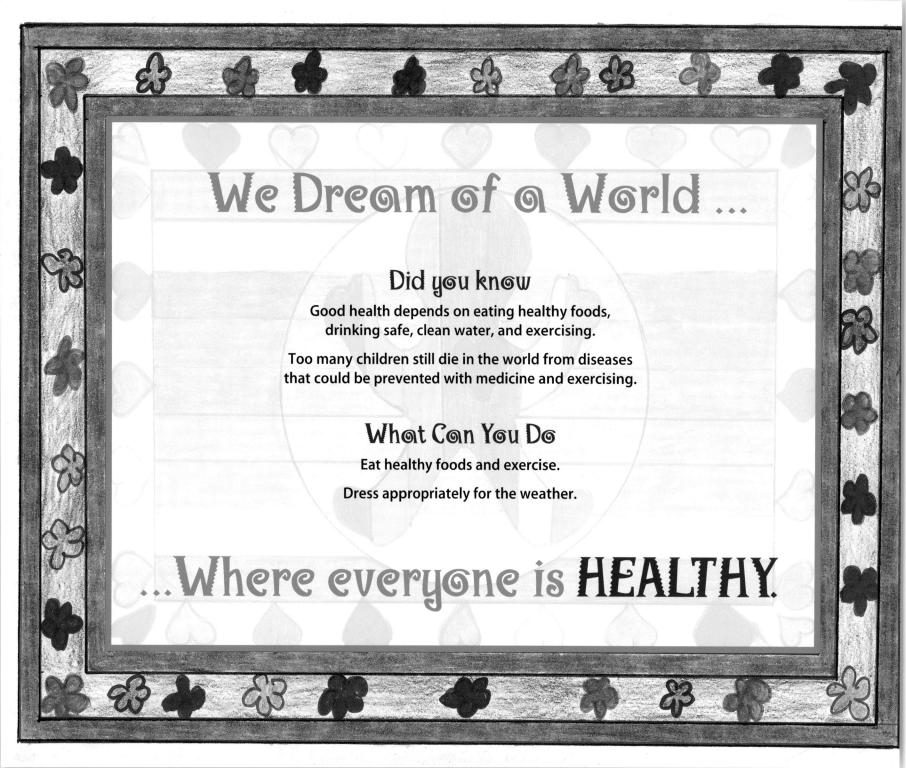

We Dream of a World ...

Did you know

Good health depends on eating healthy foods, drinking safe, clean water, and exercising.

Too many children still die in the world from diseases that could be prevented with medicine and exercising.

What Can You Do

Eat healthy foods and exercise.

Dress appropriately for the weather.

...Where everyone is HEALTHY.

We Dream of a World ...

Did you know

Everyone in the world does not read or write.

Reading helps people become knowledgeable about the world, near or far.

What Can You Do

Teach someone to read.

Sponsor a book drive and donate the books to a school or a home for children.

...Where everyone has an EDUCATION.

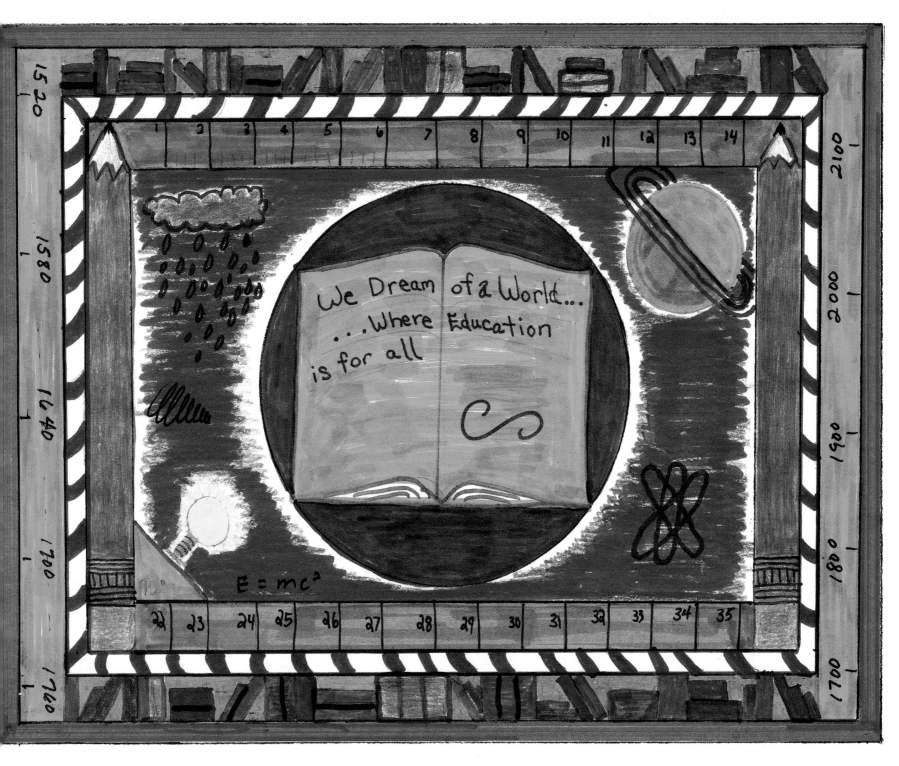

We Dream of a World ...

Did you know

Pollution causes some people to get allergies.

Pollution puts harmful chemicals in our environment.

What Can You Do

Encourage your family and friends to carpool.

Write letters to your congressman on pollution.

Buy products that are ecologically friendly.

...Where there is no
POLLUTION.

We Dream of a World ...

Did you know

Every living thing needs water.

Our drinking water comes from lakes, rivers, streams and under the ground water called groundwater. Groundwater can easily become polluted when chemical products, like paint and oil, spill and leak into the ground.

When forests are cut down, springs and underground lakes dry up. This is not good.

A seven minute shower uses about 35 gallons of water.

What Can You Do

Be a water-saver and leak detective around your house.

Tell your family and friends about the dangers of harmful spills on the ground.

Help as many people as you can learn ways to protect our waters.

... Where RIVERS and OCEANS are clean.

We Dream of a World ...

Did you know

Bio-diversity, which means variety of life, refers to the millions of fascinating species of plants and animals that live on Earth. All together we balance our world.

Each week many different kinds of species become extinct.
They vanish from Earth forever.

What Can You Do

Continue to learn and teach others about how endangered species contribute to our world.

...Where there is no threat to
ENDANGERED SPECIES.

We Dream of a World ...

Did you know

Some people are upset because some countries have much, much more than they need, while others have so little.

What Can You Do

Think about what you do and how that affects the whole world.

Share your thoughts and ideas and be willing to listen to others.

Talk problems out instead of using violence.

Where there is PEACE for all.

We Dream of a World ...

Where stars are bright.

Where skies shine blue.

Where the moon lightens our night.

Where the sun brightens our day.

Where our dreams and our hopes

Lead a bright and shiny way.

Where DREAMS come true.

It's now your turn.

On the following pages,
dream of how you can make
the world a better place...

We Dream of a World ...

We Dream of a World ...

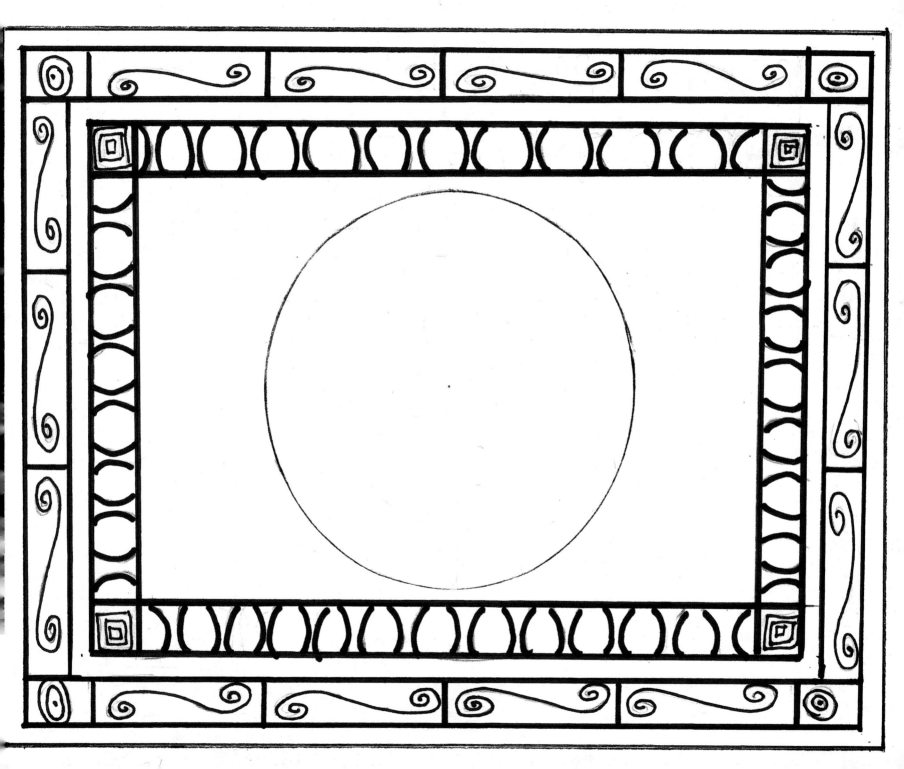

We Dream of a World ...